A World of Words: Language Education for Immigrants and Refugees Made Accessible

Boris

Copyright © [2023]

Title: A World of Words: Language Education for Immigrants and Refugees Made Accessible

Author's: Boris.

All rights reserved. No part of this publication may be reproduced, stored in a retrieval system, or transmitted in any form or by any means, electronic, mechanical, photocopying, recording, or otherwise, without the prior written permission of the publisher or author, except in the case of brief quotations embodied in critical reviews and certain other non-commercial uses permitted by copyright law.

This book was printed and published by [Publisher's: Boris] in [2023]

ISBN:

TABLE OF CONTENTS

Chapter 1: Introduction to Language Education for Immigrants and Refugees   06

Understanding the Importance of Language Education

Challenges Faced by Immigrants and Refugees in Language Learning

Chapter 2: The Basics of Language Education   10

The Fundamentals of Language Learning

Common Methods and Approaches in Language Education

Chapter 3: Creating an Inclusive Language Education Environment   14

Promoting Cultural Sensitivity and Understanding

Addressing the Unique Needs of Immigrants and Refugees

Chapter 4: Language Assessment and Placement

Evaluating Language Proficiency

Determining Appropriate Language Programs and Courses

Chapter 5: Curriculum Design for Language Education   18

Developing Engaging and Effective Language Lessons

Incorporating Real-life Situations and Contexts

Chapter 6: Teaching Strategies for Language Education   22

Interactive and Communicative Approaches

Utilizing Technology in Language Learning

Chapter 7: Supporting Immigrants and Refugees in Language Learning   26

Providing Resources and Support Services

Collaborating with Community Organizations and Volunteers

Chapter 8: Overcoming Language Barriers in Education   31

Strategies for Overcoming Language Barriers in Schools

Promoting Inclusive Education Practices

Chapter 9: Promoting Language Education for Empowerment   36

Enhancing Job Prospects and Economic Opportunities

Fostering Social Integration and Community Engagement

Chapter 10: Future Directions in Language Education for Immigrants and Refugees   40

Emerging Trends and Innovations in Language Education

Advocacy and Policy Recommendations for Language Education

Chapter 11: Conclusion   44

Recap of Key Points

Chapter 1: Introduction to Language Education for Immigrants and Refugees

Understanding the Importance of Language Education

Language education plays a crucial role in the lives of immigrants and refugees, as it is the key to communication, integration, and empowerment in their new communities. In this subchapter, we will delve into the significance of language education, highlighting how it benefits individuals and the broader society.

For immigrants and refugees, language education is the bridge that connects them to their new surroundings. It equips them with the necessary skills to communicate effectively, express their needs, and engage in various aspects of daily life. Without language proficiency, individuals may face difficulties in finding employment, accessing healthcare, or participating in civic activities. Language education provides them with the tools to navigate these challenges and foster a sense of belonging in their adopted homeland.

Language education is not only about language acquisition; it also promotes cultural understanding and appreciation. By learning the language of their host country, immigrants and refugees gain insights into the customs, traditions, and values that shape the society around them. This knowledge fosters empathy and cultural competence, enabling them to form meaningful connections with their neighbors and build bridges across diverse communities. Language education thus acts as a catalyst for social cohesion and integration.

Furthermore, language education empowers individuals to fully participate in their communities and pursue their goals. Proficiency in the local language opens doors to educational opportunities, career advancements, and economic mobility. It enhances their self-confidence and enables them to advocate for their rights and interests. Language education equips immigrants and refugees with the skills necessary to navigate the complexities of their new environment and actively contribute to the development of their communities.

From a broader perspective, language education is beneficial to the host society as well. It promotes social harmony by breaking down communication barriers and facilitating intercultural dialogue. It fosters a sense of inclusion and equal opportunities for all, contributing to the overall well-being and prosperity of the community. Language education also enriches the cultural landscape, as immigrants and refugees bring their languages, traditions, and perspectives, enhancing diversity and intercultural exchange.

In conclusion, understanding the importance of language education is paramount for both immigrants and refugees, as well as the wider society. It empowers individuals, facilitates integration, and fosters social cohesion. By investing in language education, we can create a world where language is not a barrier, but a tool for unity and mutual understanding.

Challenges Faced by Immigrants and Refugees in Language Learning

Language is not just a tool for communication; it is also a gateway to cultural integration, economic opportunities, and social inclusion. For immigrants and refugees, learning the language of their new home country is essential for their successful integration into society. However, the journey of language learning can be fraught with challenges and obstacles that can make this process overwhelming.

One of the primary challenges faced by immigrants and refugees in language learning is the sheer complexity and unfamiliarity of the new language. Many immigrants come from countries where English, for example, is not commonly spoken. Therefore, they may have little to no prior exposure to the language, making it difficult to comprehend and communicate effectively. The linguistic differences in grammar, vocabulary, and pronunciation can be daunting, leading to frustration and a sense of isolation.

Moreover, the lack of access to quality language education resources and programs can hinder the language learning process. Immigrants and refugees often face financial constraints, limited educational opportunities, and a lack of specialized language courses tailored to their specific needs. This lack of support can further exacerbate the challenges they face, making it harder for them to acquire the necessary language skills to navigate their new environment.

Additionally, cultural and social barriers can impede language learning. Immigrants and refugees may find it challenging to immerse themselves in the new culture due to cultural differences and discrimination. Discrimination can lead to feelings of self-doubt and low self-esteem, making it difficult for individuals to confidently engage in language learning activities. Cultural differences can also affect language comprehension, as idiomatic expressions, slang, and cultural references may be unfamiliar to them.

Furthermore, the trauma and stress experienced by immigrants and refugees due to their displacement or migration can also impact language learning. The emotional toll of leaving one's home country, family, and familiar surroundings can affect concentration, memory, and motivation – all crucial aspects of language acquisition.

Addressing these challenges requires a multi-faceted approach that involves the collaboration of various stakeholders. Governments, educational institutions, and community organizations must work together to provide accessible and affordable language education programs. These programs should be culturally sensitive, recognizing the unique needs and backgrounds of immigrants and refugees. Additionally, initiatives to promote inclusivity and combat discrimination are essential to creating an environment conducive to language learning.

In conclusion, the challenges faced by immigrants and refugees in language learning are numerous and complex. However, with the right support, resources, and inclusive policies, we can empower these individuals to overcome these obstacles and embrace the transformative power of language education. By doing so, we not only promote their integration into society but also foster a more inclusive and diverse community for all.

Chapter 2: The Basics of Language Education

The Fundamentals of Language Learning

Language learning is a transformative journey that opens up countless opportunities for personal growth and global connectivity. In the modern world, where multiculturalism is becoming the norm, the ability to communicate effectively in different languages is increasingly essential. Whether you are an immigrant seeking to integrate into a new society or a refugee striving to rebuild your life, language education is the key to success.

This subchapter, "The Fundamentals of Language Learning," explores the core principles and strategies that underpin effective language acquisition. It is designed to serve as a comprehensive guide for language learners of all backgrounds, ages, and proficiency levels.

First and foremost, language learning requires dedication and perseverance. It is crucial to set realistic goals and maintain a consistent study routine. Immersion in the target language is highly recommended, as it exposes learners to real-life situations and promotes active engagement with native speakers.

Building a strong foundation in grammar and vocabulary is another fundamental aspect of language learning. Grammar provides the structural framework for communication, while vocabulary allows learners to express themselves fluently. A systematic approach to learning grammar rules and expanding vocabulary through contextualized exercises is indispensable.

Listening and speaking skills are the cornerstones of effective communication. Actively listening to authentic materials, such as podcasts, songs, and movies, helps learners familiarize themselves with native pronunciation and intonation. Engaging in conversation with native speakers, whether through language exchange programs or language schools, provides an invaluable opportunity to practice speaking skills in a supportive environment.

Reading and writing skills are equally important components of language learning. Reading exposes learners to different writing styles, expands their vocabulary, and enhances their understanding of grammar. Writing, on the other hand, allows learners to apply their knowledge and express their thoughts in a structured manner. Regular practice of both skills is essential for well-rounded language proficiency.

Lastly, technology has revolutionized language learning, making it more accessible and interactive than ever before. Language learning apps, online platforms, and virtual classrooms offer a wide range of resources and tools that cater to different learning styles and preferences. Utilizing these technological advancements can greatly enhance the language acquisition process.

In conclusion, language learning is a lifelong journey that requires commitment, patience, and an open mind. By understanding and applying the fundamentals discussed in this subchapter, learners can embark on a rewarding language education experience. Whether you are an immigrant, refugee, or simply someone interested in expanding your linguistic horizons, this subchapter will serve as your compass in navigating the world of language learning.

Common Methods and Approaches in Language Education

Language education plays a vital role in helping immigrants and refugees integrate into their new communities. It provides them with the necessary skills to communicate effectively, understand cultural nuances, and navigate their daily lives. In this subchapter, we will explore some common methods and approaches used in language education to make the learning process accessible and effective for all.

One of the most widely used methods is the communicative approach, which focuses on developing students' ability to use language for real-life purposes. This approach encourages students to engage in meaningful conversations, role-plays, and interactive activities that simulate authentic language use. By immersing students in practical situations, they gain confidence and proficiency in their new language.

Another popular method is the task-based approach, where language learning is integrated into completing specific tasks or projects. This approach promotes active learning and allows students to apply their language skills in real-world contexts. Students might work collaboratively to solve problems, conduct interviews, or create presentations, thereby enhancing their language proficiency while achieving tangible goals.

In addition to these methods, technology has revolutionized language education. Online platforms, language learning apps, and virtual classrooms have made language learning more accessible and engaging. These tools provide opportunities for interactive learning, self-paced study, and personalized feedback. Integrating technology into language education allows learners to practice their skills independently and receive immediate support when needed.

Furthermore, the inclusion of cultural components is crucial in language education. Understanding cultural norms, traditions, and social etiquette helps learners become more culturally competent and effective communicators. Incorporating cultural activities, such as cooking classes, field trips, or storytelling sessions, fosters appreciation for diverse backgrounds and encourages dialogue among students.

Lastly, differentiated instruction is essential in catering to the individual needs and learning styles of students. By adapting teaching methods, materials, and assessments to accommodate diverse learners, language educators create inclusive and supportive environments. Differentiated instruction might involve providing visual aids, offering additional practice opportunities, or using multimedia resources to cater to various learning preferences.

In conclusion, language education for immigrants and refugees should encompass a variety of methods and approaches to ensure accessibility and effectiveness. The communicative and task-based approaches foster practical language skills, while technology enhances engagement and independent learning. Cultural components and differentiated instruction promote inclusivity and address individual needs. By employing these methods and approaches, language educators can create a world of words that is accessible and beneficial for all learners.

Chapter 3: Creating an Inclusive Language Education Environment

Promoting Cultural Sensitivity and Understanding

In today's interconnected world, cultural diversity is becoming increasingly evident in our communities. As language educators, it is our responsibility to foster an environment that promotes cultural sensitivity and understanding. By embracing diversity and encouraging open-mindedness, we can create a more inclusive and harmonious society for everyone.

Cultural sensitivity refers to the awareness and appreciation of different cultural norms, values, and traditions. It involves recognizing and respecting the unique perspectives and experiences that individuals from various cultures bring to the table. By promoting cultural sensitivity in our language education programs, we can help immigrants and refugees feel validated and accepted in their new communities.

Understanding is the key to building bridges between different cultures. By encouraging dialogue and open communication, we can break down barriers and promote mutual understanding. Language education provides an ideal platform for this exchange, as it allows individuals from different backgrounds to learn from one another and develop empathy for each other's experiences.

There are several strategies that language educators can employ to promote cultural sensitivity and understanding in their classrooms. Firstly, it is crucial to create a safe and inclusive learning environment where all students feel valued and respected. This can be achieved by encouraging open discussions about cultural differences and fostering a sense of curiosity and appreciation for diversity.

Additionally, incorporating cultural content into the curriculum can enrich the learning experience for students. By introducing literature, music, and art from different cultures, educators can expose students to a variety of perspectives and promote understanding. This can also help students connect with their own cultural heritage and build a sense of pride and identity.

Furthermore, promoting cultural sensitivity and understanding requires educators to be mindful of their own biases and assumptions. It is essential to approach teaching with an open mind and to continuously educate ourselves about different cultures. By being aware of our own biases, we can avoid perpetuating stereotypes and create a more inclusive learning environment.

In conclusion, promoting cultural sensitivity and understanding is vital in language education for immigrants and refugees. By fostering a safe and inclusive environment, incorporating cultural content into the curriculum, and being mindful of our own biases, we can help build bridges between different cultures and create a more harmonious society for everyone. Language education has the power to unite people from diverse backgrounds and contribute to a world where diversity is celebrated and respected.

Addressing the Unique Needs of Immigrants and Refugees

In today's globalized world, language education plays a crucial role in facilitating the integration and empowerment of immigrants and refugees. As diverse populations continue to migrate across borders, it is essential to recognize and address the unique needs that these individuals face when it comes to language learning.

Immigrants and refugees often arrive in a new country with limited or no knowledge of the local language. This language barrier can be a significant obstacle to their successful integration into their new communities. Recognizing this, language education programs have a responsibility to provide tailored instruction that takes into account the specific challenges faced by immigrants and refugees.

One of the key considerations in addressing the unique needs of immigrants and refugees is understanding their diverse backgrounds and experiences. Immigrants and refugees come from a wide range of countries, cultures, and linguistic backgrounds. Therefore, language educators must adopt an inclusive and multicultural approach to their teaching methods. This includes incorporating culturally relevant content, celebrating diversity, and creating a safe and welcoming learning environment.

Furthermore, language education programs must be equipped to support the linguistic and educational needs of immigrants and refugees. Many individuals may have had interrupted or limited access to formal education in their home countries due to conflict or displacement. Language educators must be prepared to provide foundational literacy and numeracy skills to bridge these gaps.

Additionally, language education for immigrants and refugees should focus on practical language skills that are immediately applicable to their daily lives. This includes teaching functional vocabulary for accessing basic services, navigating public transportation, and finding employment. By equipping immigrants and refugees with these skills, language education programs can empower them to become active participants in their new communities.

Addressing the unique needs of immigrants and refugees also involves fostering social connections and building support networks. Language education programs should create opportunities for language learners to interact with native speakers, engage in community activities, and participate in language exchange programs. These experiences not only enhance language learning but also help immigrants and refugees build social connections, reduce isolation, and gain a sense of belonging.

In conclusion, language education for immigrants and refugees must be designed to address their unique needs. By adopting an inclusive and multicultural approach, providing foundational skills, focusing on practical language skills, and fostering social connections, language education programs can empower immigrants and refugees to navigate their new environments successfully. Language education plays a crucial role in ensuring that immigrants and refugees can fully participate in their new communities, contribute to society, and achieve their goals in their adopted countries. It is our collective responsibility to make language education accessible and inclusive for every individual, regardless of their background or circumstances.

Chapter 4: Language Assessment and Placement

Evaluating Language Proficiency

In the diverse and interconnected world we live in, language education plays a crucial role in facilitating communication and integration for immigrants and refugees. The ability to effectively communicate in a new language opens up doors to employment, education, and social interaction. However, evaluating language proficiency can be a complex task that requires careful consideration and a comprehensive approach.

When it comes to evaluating language proficiency, it is important to take into account the unique needs and backgrounds of individuals. Every learner brings their own experiences, skills, and challenges to the language learning journey. Therefore, a one-size-fits-all approach may not be suitable. Instead, language educators should employ a variety of assessment methods to accurately gauge language proficiency.

One commonly used assessment tool is the Common European Framework of Reference for Languages (CEFR). This framework provides a standardized way of measuring language proficiency across different languages and proficiency levels. By using the CEFR, language educators can evaluate learners' reading, writing, listening, and speaking skills, and assign them a level ranging from A1 (beginner) to C2 (proficient). This allows educators to tailor their instruction to meet the specific needs of each learner.

In addition to standardized assessments, it is essential to consider real-life language use when evaluating proficiency. Language proficiency goes beyond mere grammar and vocabulary knowledge. It encompasses the ability to understand and express oneself in various social and cultural contexts. Therefore, incorporating authentic tasks and situational exercises in assessments can provide a more accurate reflection of learners' language abilities.

Furthermore, evaluating language proficiency should not be a one-time event. It is an ongoing process that requires continuous assessment and feedback. Regular check-ins and progress evaluations can help learners track their development and identify areas for improvement. Additionally, incorporating self-assessment tools empowers learners to take responsibility for their own progress and set realistic goals.

Overall, evaluating language proficiency in the context of language education for immigrants and refugees requires a multifaceted approach. By combining standardized assessments, real-life language use, and ongoing evaluation, language educators can effectively gauge learners' abilities and tailor instruction accordingly. This comprehensive assessment approach promotes inclusivity, empowers learners, and ensures that language education remains accessible and beneficial for everyone.

Determining Appropriate Language Programs and Courses

In today's diverse and interconnected world, language education plays a crucial role in ensuring effective communication and integration for immigrants and refugees. However, with the abundance of language programs and courses available, it can be challenging to determine the most suitable option for each individual's needs. This subchapter aims to guide individuals seeking language education, providing valuable insights on how to choose appropriate programs and courses.

First and foremost, it is essential to assess one's language proficiency level. This evaluation enables prospective learners to identify their strengths and weaknesses and determine the appropriate starting point for their language journey. Numerous language assessment tools and tests are available, such as the Common European Framework of Reference for Languages (CEFR), which provides a standardized framework for language proficiency.

Once the language proficiency level has been established, the next step is to consider the specific goals and objectives of language learning. For immigrants and refugees, language education often revolves around acquiring practical language skills for daily life, employment, or further education. Therefore, it is crucial to choose programs and courses that align with these objectives. For example, if the goal is to enhance employability, selecting a program that emphasizes workplace communication skills would be highly advantageous.

Another crucial factor to consider is the teaching methodology employed by the language program or course. Different individuals have varying learning styles and preferences. Some may thrive in a classroom setting, while others may prefer independent study or online platforms. It is important to choose a program that utilizes teaching methods that resonate with the learner's style, ensuring optimal engagement and progress.

Financial considerations also play a significant role in determining suitable language programs and courses. While some individuals may have access to government-funded programs or scholarships, others may need to explore affordable options. Community centers, nonprofit organizations, and online platforms often offer language courses at more accessible rates, ensuring that language education remains accessible to all.

Lastly, it is crucial to seek out programs and courses that foster inclusivity and cultural sensitivity. Immigrants and refugees often face unique challenges related to language learning, and it is vital to choose programs that provide adequate support and understanding. Look for programs that incorporate cultural awareness, provide resources for language learners from diverse backgrounds, and prioritize inclusivity in their curriculum.

By considering these factors, individuals seeking language education can make informed decisions and select programs and courses that cater to their specific needs and goals. Language education is a powerful tool that empowers immigrants and refugees, enabling them to fully participate in their new communities and navigate their new lives with confidence and proficiency.

Chapter 5: Curriculum Design for Language Education

Developing Engaging and Effective Language Lessons

In the realm of language education, the key to success lies in creating engaging and effective lessons that captivate learners and facilitate their language acquisition journey. Whether you are a language teacher, an aspiring educator, or simply interested in improving your own language skills, this subchapter will provide you with valuable insights and practical strategies to make your language lessons both engaging and effective.

One of the fundamental principles in developing engaging language lessons is to create a student-centered learning environment. This means shifting the focus from the teacher as the sole provider of knowledge to actively involving learners in the learning process. By incorporating interactive activities, group work, and multimedia resources, students are given the opportunity to actively engage with the language and practice their skills in a meaningful context.

Another important aspect to consider is the use of authentic materials. Immigrants and refugees often face the challenge of adapting to a new culture and language, so incorporating real-life materials such as newspaper articles, songs, and videos not only enhances their language skills but also exposes them to the cultural nuances of their new environment. This approach allows learners to see the practical applications of the language they are learning and fosters a deeper understanding of the language in context.

Furthermore, integrating technology into language lessons can greatly enhance engagement and effectiveness. The use of online resources, language learning apps, and interactive platforms can create a dynamic and interactive learning experience. Additionally, technology allows for personalized learning, where learners can progress at their own pace and focus on areas that need improvement.

In order to ensure that language lessons are effective, it is crucial to regularly assess and evaluate students' progress. This can be done through formative assessments, such as quizzes and assignments, as well as summative assessments, like tests and projects. By providing timely feedback, teachers can identify areas for improvement and tailor their instruction to meet the specific needs of each learner.

In conclusion, developing engaging and effective language lessons requires a student-centered approach, the use of authentic materials, integration of technology, and regular assessment. By implementing these strategies, language educators and learners alike can embark on a fruitful language acquisition journey. Remember, language education is a lifelong process, and with the right tools and techniques, everyone can unlock the world of words and thrive in their new linguistic environment.

Incorporating Real-life Situations and Contexts

In the pursuit of effective language education for immigrants and refugees, it is crucial to incorporate real-life situations and contexts into the learning process. This subchapter explores the significance of integrating authentic experiences and practical scenarios into language learning programs, ensuring that every learner can develop the necessary skills to thrive in their new environment.

Language education is not just about memorizing vocabulary and grammar rules; it is about empowering individuals to communicate effectively in their daily lives. By incorporating real-life situations and contexts, learners are presented with opportunities to apply their language skills in practical ways. This approach enhances their ability to understand and respond to real-world situations, whether it be ordering food at a restaurant, asking for directions, or engaging in meaningful conversations with others.

One of the key advantages of incorporating real-life situations is the development of functional language skills. Language learners need to be equipped with the ability to navigate the intricacies of their new society, and this can only be achieved through exposure to authentic situations. By simulating real-life scenarios, educators can guide learners in developing the necessary vocabulary, grammatical structures, and cultural awareness needed to communicate effectively in various contexts.

Additionally, incorporating real-life situations and contexts promotes learner engagement and motivation. It provides learners with a sense of purpose and relevance, as they can see the immediate practicality of the language skills they are acquiring. When learners understand that the language they are learning has direct applications to their daily lives, they become more motivated to actively participate and invest in their learning journey.

Furthermore, incorporating real-life situations and contexts fosters cultural integration. Immigrants and refugees often face challenges in adapting to a new culture, and language education plays a vital role in this process. By exposing learners to real-life situations, they gain a deeper understanding of the cultural nuances and expectations of their new environment. This understanding not only facilitates their integration but also promotes empathy, respect, and intercultural communication.

In conclusion, incorporating real-life situations and contexts into language education programs is essential for the successful integration and empowerment of immigrants and refugees. By providing learners with opportunities to apply their language skills in practical ways, educators can help them develop functional language skills, enhance their motivation, and foster cultural integration. This approach ensures that language education becomes accessible and relevant to all learners, enabling them to thrive in their new world of words.

Chapter 6: Teaching Strategies for Language Education

Interactive and Communicative Approaches

In today's globalized world, effective communication is more important than ever. For immigrants and refugees seeking to learn a new language, interactive and communicative approaches are crucial to mastering the language skills needed to succeed in their new communities. This subchapter explores the importance of these approaches in language education, providing valuable insights and strategies for educators and learners alike.

Interactive approaches in language education focus on creating an engaging and dynamic learning environment. Instead of relying solely on textbooks and lectures, interactive methods encourage active participation and collaboration. This can include group discussions, role-playing exercises, and interactive multimedia materials. By incorporating these methods into language classes, educators can create an immersive and stimulating learning experience that encourages students to practice their language skills in real-life situations.

Communicative approaches, on the other hand, prioritize the development of practical communication skills. Rather than focusing solely on grammar and vocabulary, communicative language teaching emphasizes the ability to express oneself and understand others in real-world contexts. This approach encourages learners to engage in meaningful interactions and provides opportunities for authentic communication in the target language. Through role-plays, simulations, and language games, students can practice their speaking, listening, reading, and writing skills while gaining confidence and fluency.

The benefits of interactive and communicative approaches in language education are numerous. Firstly, these approaches foster a learner-centered environment, where the students take an active role in their language learning journey. By allowing students to participate and contribute to the learning process, educators can create a sense of ownership and motivation that accelerates language acquisition.

Additionally, interactive and communicative approaches promote cultural understanding and integration. Through interactive activities, students can explore different perspectives, share their own experiences, and develop empathy for others. This not only enhances their language skills but also fosters a sense of community and acceptance.

Moreover, these approaches prepare learners for real-life situations. By practicing communication in authentic contexts, students gain the confidence and skills necessary to navigate their new environment. Whether it's ordering food at a restaurant, making small talk with neighbors, or participating in job interviews, interactive and communicative approaches provide learners with the practical tools they need to thrive in their new language.

In conclusion, interactive and communicative approaches are essential in language education for immigrants and refugees. By creating interactive and engaging learning environments and prioritizing practical communication skills, educators can empower language learners to effectively communicate and integrate into their new communities. These approaches not only enhance language skills but also promote cultural understanding and prepare learners for real-life situations. Whether you are an educator or a language learner, incorporating interactive and communicative approaches into your language education journey will undoubtedly lead to successful language acquisition.

Utilizing Technology in Language Learning

In today's digital age, technology has become an integral part of our daily lives. From smartphones to tablets, there is no denying that technology has revolutionized the way we communicate, learn, and access information. Language education is no exception to this trend. In fact, technology can play a crucial role in making language learning more accessible, engaging, and effective for immigrants and refugees.

One of the key advantages of utilizing technology in language learning is the accessibility it provides. With the proliferation of online platforms, individuals from every corner of the globe can now access language learning resources at their own convenience. Whether it's through interactive language learning apps, online courses, or virtual language exchange programs, technology has made it possible for anyone with an internet connection to embark on their language learning journey.

Furthermore, technology offers a wide range of tools and resources that can enhance the language learning experience. With language learning apps, learners can practice vocabulary, grammar, and pronunciation through interactive exercises and games. Online platforms also provide access to authentic language materials such as podcasts, videos, and news articles, allowing learners to immerse themselves in real-world language contexts.

Another benefit of technology in language education is its ability to foster engagement and motivation. Gamification elements, such as leaderboards, badges, and rewards, can make language learning more enjoyable and encourage learners to stay motivated. Virtual language exchange programs provide opportunities for learners to connect with native speakers around the world, enabling them to practice their language skills in a supportive and authentic environment.

Moreover, technology can facilitate personalized learning experiences. Adaptive learning platforms can tailor lessons and exercises based on learners' individual needs and progress, ensuring that they receive targeted instruction and practice. Language learning apps also allow learners to set goals, track their progress, and receive instant feedback, enabling them to monitor their improvement and stay motivated.

However, it is important to note that technology should not replace human interaction in language learning. While technology can provide valuable resources and tools, face-to-face communication and interaction with teachers and peers remain essential for language acquisition. A blended approach that combines technology with traditional classroom instruction can ensure a well-rounded language learning experience.

In conclusion, technology has the power to revolutionize language education for immigrants and refugees. By leveraging the accessibility, resources, engagement, and personalization that technology offers, individuals from all walks of life can embark on a language learning journey that suits their needs and aspirations. Embracing technology in language education can empower learners and provide them with the skills they need to thrive in their new homes.

Chapter 7: Supporting Immigrants and Refugees in Language Learning

Providing Resources and Support Services

In the challenging journey of language education for immigrants and refugees, it is vital to have access to resources and support services that can help facilitate their integration into their new communities. This subchapter aims to highlight the importance of providing such resources and services and how they can contribute to a more accessible language education experience.

1. Language Learning Materials: Immigrants and refugees often face barriers when it comes to accessing language learning materials. It is crucial to offer a wide range of resources, such as textbooks, online courses, and language apps, to cater to diverse learning styles and preferences. These materials should be designed to be user-friendly and culturally sensitive, ensuring that learners feel comfortable and engaged during their language learning journey.

2. Community Centers and Language Schools: Establishing community centers and language schools that specialize in language education for immigrants and refugees can significantly enhance their learning experience. These centers should provide a supportive and inclusive environment where learners can practice their language skills and receive guidance from qualified instructors. Additionally, organizing cultural events and workshops can help foster a sense of belonging and encourage learners to embrace their new language and culture.

3. Tutoring and Mentorship Programs: Immigrants and refugees may benefit greatly from one-on-one tutoring and mentorship programs. These programs can pair learners with experienced individuals who can provide personalized guidance, support, and motivation. Mentors can also help learners navigate their new surroundings, including finding employment opportunities and accessing social services, further enhancing their integration process.

4. Counseling and Mental Health Services: The language education journey can be emotionally challenging for immigrants and refugees. Providing access to counseling and mental health services is crucial to ensuring their overall well-being and success in language learning. These services should be culturally sensitive, addressing the unique challenges and traumas that learners may have experienced in their home countries or during their migration.

5. Collaboration with Community Organizations: Collaborating with community organizations that specialize in immigrant and refugee support can expand the range of resources and services available to language learners. These organizations often have extensive networks and expertise in areas such as employment assistance, housing, legal aid, and healthcare. By working together, language education providers can offer comprehensive support to learners, addressing their holistic needs.

In conclusion, providing resources and support services is essential for making language education accessible to immigrants and refugees. By offering a wide range of learning materials, establishing community centers and language schools, implementing tutoring and mentorship programs, providing counseling and mental health services, and collaborating with community organizations, language education providers can create an inclusive and supportive environment that empowers learners to thrive in their new communities.

Collaborating with Community Organizations and Volunteers

In the realm of language education for immigrants and refugees, collaboration with community organizations and volunteers is an invaluable resource. This subchapter aims to shed light on the importance of such collaborations and how they can significantly enhance the learning experience for individuals seeking to acquire a new language.

Community organizations play a vital role in supporting language education initiatives. These organizations often have a deep understanding of the needs and challenges faced by immigrant and refugee communities. By partnering with them, language educators can tap into their expertise, resources, and network of support. For instance, community organizations can help identify specific language learning needs within the community, offer cultural insights, and facilitate access to additional resources such as textbooks, technology, or funding opportunities.

Furthermore, community organizations can provide a bridge between language learners and the wider community. By organizing cultural exchange programs, social events, or community service projects, learners can apply their language skills in real-life situations, fostering a sense of belonging and connection. These interactions also allow learners to practice their language skills with native speakers, accelerating their language acquisition process.

Volunteers are another valuable asset in the field of language education. Individuals who possess language skills, cultural knowledge, or teaching experience can make a profound impact on the learning journey of immigrants and refugees. Volunteers can assist in facilitating language classes, leading conversation groups, or providing one-on-one tutoring sessions. Their dedication and passion can create a supportive and encouraging learning environment, helping learners build confidence and motivation.

Moreover, volunteers can bring diverse perspectives and experiences to the classroom, enriching the learning experience for everyone involved. By sharing their personal stories, volunteers can help learners gain a deeper understanding of different cultures and foster empathy and tolerance.

In conclusion, collaborating with community organizations and volunteers is essential in creating a comprehensive and inclusive language education program for immigrants and refugees. The involvement of community organizations can provide valuable insights, resources, and support, while volunteers can offer language skills, cultural knowledge, and a sense of connection. By harnessing the power of collaboration, language educators can create an environment where language learners feel empowered, supported, and motivated to reach their full potential.

Chapter 8: Overcoming Language Barriers in Education

Strategies for Overcoming Language Barriers in Schools

In today's diverse society, schools often face the challenge of providing effective language education to immigrant and refugee students. Language barriers can hinder their academic progress and social integration, but with the right strategies in place, these barriers can be overcome. This subchapter explores various approaches that educators and administrators can adopt to make language education more accessible and inclusive for all students.

One of the key strategies is to create a supportive and inclusive learning environment. This involves fostering a sense of belonging among students, regardless of their language proficiency. Encouraging peer-to-peer interactions and collaborative learning can help break down language barriers and promote cultural exchange. Additionally, teachers can use visual aids, gestures, and real-life examples to enhance understanding and engagement.

Another important strategy is to provide targeted language support. This can be achieved by offering specialized language programs or classes that focus on developing the linguistic skills necessary for academic success. Teachers can use differentiated instruction techniques to address the diverse needs of students with varying language abilities. It is also crucial to assess students' language proficiency regularly to track their progress and adjust instruction accordingly.

Incorporating technology into language education is another effective strategy. Online resources, language learning apps, and digital platforms can supplement classroom instruction and provide students with additional opportunities for practice. Technology can also facilitate communication between teachers, students, and parents, ensuring a collaborative approach to language learning.

Collaboration with families and communities is a vital aspect of overcoming language barriers in schools. Engaging parents and caregivers in their children's education can help create a support network that extends beyond the classroom. Schools can offer language classes or workshops for families, encouraging them to maintain their native language while also learning the dominant language of their new environment.

Professional development for educators is crucial to implement effective language education strategies. Providing teachers with training and resources on language acquisition theories, instructional strategies, and cultural competence can enhance their ability to address language barriers in the classroom.

By implementing these strategies, schools can create an inclusive and accessible language education environment for immigrant and refugee students. This not only supports their academic success but also promotes their social integration and overall well-being. Language barriers should never be a hindrance to learning, and with the right approaches, every student can thrive in a world of words.

Promoting Inclusive Education Practices

In today's multicultural and diverse society, it is crucial to ensure that every individual has equal access to quality education. This subchapter, "Promoting Inclusive Education Practices," explores the importance of creating inclusive learning environments for immigrants and refugees in the field of language education.

Inclusive education practices aim to create an environment where every student feels valued, respected, and supported, regardless of their cultural or linguistic background. By promoting inclusivity, we foster a sense of belonging and empower individuals to achieve their full potential.

Language education plays a pivotal role in the integration and success of immigrants and refugees in their new communities. It provides them with the necessary tools to communicate effectively, participate actively, and navigate their surroundings with confidence. However, to ensure the effectiveness of language education, it is essential to adopt inclusive practices.

One fundamental aspect of inclusive language education is recognizing and embracing students' diverse backgrounds. Educators should acknowledge the cultural, linguistic, and experiential differences among learners and use these as valuable resources in the classroom. By incorporating students' diverse experiences, we create a rich and dynamic learning environment that benefits all.

Another crucial element of inclusive education practices is fostering a sense of community and collaboration. Creating opportunities for students to engage in group work, peer learning, and cultural exchange not only enhances language skills but also promotes understanding, empathy, and appreciation for different cultures. By facilitating interactions among students from diverse backgrounds, we encourage mutual respect and the breaking down of barriers.

Furthermore, inclusive education practices prioritize differentiated instruction. Recognizing that learners have varied needs, abilities, and learning styles, educators should employ a range of teaching strategies and resources to cater to individual differences. This approach ensures that every student can actively participate and progress at their own pace.

Inclusive language education also involves involving families, communities, and support networks in the learning process. By establishing strong partnerships with parents, community organizations, and social services, educators can better understand the unique needs of their students and provide appropriate support. Collaborating with these stakeholders helps create a holistic approach to education, ensuring that students receive comprehensive support both inside and outside the classroom.

In conclusion, promoting inclusive education practices in the field of language education is crucial for the successful integration and empowerment of immigrants and refugees. By recognizing and embracing diversity, fostering collaboration, differentiating instruction, and involving families and communities, we can create inclusive learning environments where every individual thrives. These practices not only cultivate language skills but also foster empathy, understanding, and a sense of belonging, ultimately contributing to a more inclusive and cohesive society.

Chapter 9: Promoting Language Education for Empowerment

Enhancing Job Prospects and Economic Opportunities

In today's globalized world, language education plays a crucial role in opening up new doors of opportunities for immigrants and refugees. The ability to communicate effectively in the language of their host country not only enhances their job prospects but also boosts their economic integration and overall well-being.

Language education is the key that can unlock a world of possibilities. When immigrants and refugees are equipped with the necessary language skills, they can confidently navigate the job market, engage in meaningful conversations, and build relationships with employers and colleagues. By understanding the nuances of the local language, they become better equipped to showcase their talents, skills, and qualifications, making them more competitive in the job market.

Employers increasingly value multilingual employees for their ability to bridge cultural gaps, communicate with diverse customers, and contribute to a globalized workforce. By investing in language education, immigrants and refugees can enhance their employability, increase their earning potential, and secure stable employment. A proficient command of the language of their host country enables them to access a wider range of job opportunities, thereby empowering them to contribute to society and achieve economic stability.

Moreover, language education is not limited to job prospects alone. It also opens up economic opportunities beyond traditional employment. Immigrants and refugees who possess language skills can engage in entrepreneurial endeavors, start their own businesses, and contribute to local economic growth. By harnessing their linguistic abilities, they can build bridges between their own communities and the wider society, fostering cultural exchange and economic cooperation.

Language education for immigrants and refugees should be accessible to everyone. It is crucial to provide comprehensive language programs that cater to the diverse needs of individuals, taking into account their language proficiency levels, educational backgrounds, and cultural experiences. By offering tailored language courses, vocational training, and mentorship programs, we can empower immigrants and refugees to overcome language barriers and achieve their full potential.

In conclusion, enhancing job prospects and economic opportunities through language education is vital for the successful integration of immigrants and refugees into their host societies. By equipping them with the tools to communicate effectively and confidently, we can create a more inclusive society where everyone can thrive and contribute to the economy. Let us work together to make language education accessible to all, unlocking a world of words and endless possibilities.

Fostering Social Integration and Community Engagement

In today's globalized world, language education plays a crucial role in promoting social integration and community engagement for immigrants and refugees. The ability to communicate effectively in the local language not only facilitates daily interactions but also opens doors to various opportunities, bridging cultural gaps and fostering a sense of belonging.

Language education serves as a powerful tool to empower individuals, enabling them to participate actively in their new communities. By providing immigrants and refugees with language skills, we equip them with the means to navigate the complexities of everyday life, including accessing healthcare, education, employment, and social services. Language education also enhances their ability to voice their needs, rights, and aspirations, thus promoting empowerment and self-determination.

Moreover, language education acts as a catalyst for social integration. When immigrants and refugees are proficient in the local language, they can engage in meaningful interactions with native speakers, breaking down barriers and building relationships. This fosters a sense of belonging and inclusion, promoting social cohesion and mutual understanding.

Community engagement is another key aspect of successful integration. By actively participating in community activities, immigrants and refugees can contribute their unique perspectives, skills, and experiences, enriching the social fabric. Language education equips them with the linguistic tools necessary to engage in community initiatives, volunteer work, and cultural events, thus promoting intercultural dialogue and cooperation.

To ensure effective language education for immigrants and refugees, it is essential to adopt an inclusive and accessible approach. Language programs should be designed to meet the diverse needs of learners, taking into account their linguistic backgrounds, educational levels, and individual learning styles. By providing tailored language instruction and resources, educators can create an environment conducive to learning and encourage active participation.

Furthermore, collaboration between language education providers, community organizations, and local authorities is crucial. By working together, these stakeholders can develop comprehensive integration strategies that incorporate language learning as a central component. This includes promoting multilingualism, offering language support in various settings (such as workplaces and healthcare facilities), and fostering intercultural exchange programs.

In conclusion, language education is a powerful tool for promoting social integration and community engagement among immigrants and refugees. By equipping individuals with language skills and fostering a sense of belonging, language education empowers them to actively participate in their new communities. It is crucial for educators, community organizations, and authorities to collaborate and adopt inclusive approaches to ensure effective language education that meets the diverse needs of learners. Ultimately, by promoting social integration and community engagement, we can create a more cohesive and inclusive society for all.

Chapter 10: Future Directions in Language Education for Immigrants and Refugees

Emerging Trends and Innovations in Language Education

Language education is constantly evolving to meet the needs of an ever-changing world. As the global community becomes more interconnected, the importance of effective language learning and communication skills cannot be overstated. In this subchapter, we will explore the emerging trends and innovations in language education that are transforming how we teach and learn languages.

One of the most significant trends in language education is the integration of technology in the classroom. Digital platforms and online resources have revolutionized language learning, making it more accessible and engaging for learners of all ages and backgrounds. Virtual classrooms, interactive language-learning apps, and multimedia resources have opened up new possibilities for self-paced learning and personalized instruction. These technological advancements not only enhance language acquisition but also foster cross-cultural understanding and global collaboration.

Another emerging trend in language education is a shift towards task-based and communicative approaches. Gone are the days of rote memorization and grammar drills. Language educators now emphasize the importance of practical language skills and authentic communication. Learners are encouraged to engage in real-life tasks and meaningful interactions that mirror the situations they may encounter in their daily lives. This approach promotes active participation, critical thinking, and problem-solving skills while simultaneously building confidence and fluency.

Innovative teaching methodologies such as flipped classrooms and blended learning have also gained traction in language education. Flipped classrooms invert the traditional learning model, with students accessing instructional materials online before coming to class. This allows for more interactive and collaborative activities during class time, maximizing the use of face-to-face interactions. Blended learning combines online and in-person instruction, providing learners with flexibility and individualized support.

Furthermore, language educators are increasingly recognizing the importance of multicultural and multilingual education. With the rise of migration and globalization, classrooms are becoming more diverse, with students from various linguistic and cultural backgrounds. In response, language education has shifted towards a more inclusive and culturally sensitive approach. This includes incorporating students' native languages and cultures into the curriculum, promoting intercultural competence, and fostering respect and appreciation for diversity.

In conclusion, the field of language education is experiencing exciting developments and innovations. From the integration of technology to the adoption of task-based approaches, these emerging trends are shaping the way we teach and learn languages. By embracing these advancements and cultivating a learner-centered and inclusive environment, language educators can empower individuals from all walks of life to become confident and effective communicators in a globalized world. Whether you are a language learner, teacher, or simply interested in the field, staying informed about these trends is crucial in enhancing language education for everyone.

Advocacy and Policy Recommendations for Language Education

In today's diverse and interconnected world, language education plays a crucial role in empowering immigrants and refugees to fully participate in society. Effective language education programs not only facilitate communication but also promote cultural understanding and integration. This subchapter aims to address the importance of advocacy and provide policy recommendations for enhancing language education for immigrants and refugees.

Advocacy serves as a catalyst for change, urging governments, educational institutions, and communities to prioritize language education. By raising awareness about the benefits of language education, advocates can highlight the positive impact it has on individuals and society as a whole. They can emphasize how language skills empower immigrants and refugees to access employment opportunities, further their education, and actively engage in community life.

To advocate for improved language education, individuals and organizations should collaborate and form alliances. By working together, they can amplify their voices and influence policy decisions. Advocacy efforts should focus on promoting inclusivity, diversity, and equity in language education programs. This means advocating for sufficient funding, qualified teachers, and culturally responsive materials that cater to the unique linguistic and cultural backgrounds of learners.

Policy recommendations play a crucial role in shaping language education programs. These recommendations should address the needs of diverse learner populations and emphasize the importance of multilingualism as a valuable asset in today's globalized world. The policy framework should include provisions for comprehensive language assessment, flexible learning pathways, and ongoing support for learners.

Additionally, policies should encourage collaboration between language education providers, community organizations, and employers to promote language learning opportunities beyond the classroom. Workplace language programs, community language centers, and online resources can all contribute to creating a holistic and immersive language learning experience.

It is vital for policymakers to recognize the long-term benefits of investing in language education. By facilitating language acquisition, they can foster social cohesion, reduce language barriers, and enable immigrants and refugees to fully participate in the economic, social, and cultural fabric of their new communities.

In conclusion, advocacy and policy recommendations are essential for advancing language education for immigrants and refugees. By advocating for inclusive and equitable language education, we can create a world where language is not a barrier but a bridge to integration and success. It is the responsibility of governments, educational institutions, and communities to prioritize language education and create policies that support the needs of diverse learner populations. Together, we can make language education accessible to all and build a more inclusive and interconnected society.

Chapter 11: Conclusion

Recap of Key Points

In this subchapter, we will summarize the key points discussed throughout this book, "A World of Words: Language Education for Immigrants and Refugees Made Accessible." Our aim is to provide a comprehensive overview of the essential concepts and strategies covered in the previous chapters, ensuring that readers can easily recall and apply the valuable knowledge gained.

First and foremost, we emphasized the importance of language education for immigrants and refugees. We live in a diverse world where effective communication is essential for integration, empowerment, and personal growth. Language education plays a crucial role in facilitating these processes, enabling individuals to develop the linguistic skills needed to navigate their new surroundings successfully.

We then explored various approaches and techniques for teaching languages to immigrants and refugees. From the communicative approach to task-based learning, the book offers a range of practical strategies that educators can employ to create engaging and effective language lessons. We also highlighted the significance of cultural sensitivity and inclusivity in language education, recognizing the diverse backgrounds and experiences of learners.

Another key point discussed was the importance of creating a supportive and inclusive learning environment. We delved into the significance of building rapport with learners, fostering a sense of belonging, and promoting mutual respect. By creating a safe and welcoming space, educators can facilitate the language learning process and empower learners to actively participate and take ownership of their education.

Furthermore, we explored the role of technology in language education, acknowledging its potential to enhance learning experiences. From language learning apps to online resources, technology can provide learners with additional tools and opportunities for practice. However, we also emphasized the need for a balanced approach, where technology is used as a supplement to traditional teaching methodologies.

Lastly, we discussed the importance of continuous professional development for language educators. In order to stay up-to-date with the latest research and pedagogical approaches, educators must engage in ongoing learning and professional growth. We highlighted the significance of attending conferences, participating in workshops, and staying connected with professional networks to ensure the delivery of high-quality language education.

In conclusion, this subchapter serves as a recap of the key points covered throughout "A World of Words: Language Education for Immigrants and Refugees Made Accessible." By revisiting these crucial concepts, we hope to reinforce the essential knowledge and strategies required to create inclusive and effective language education programs. Whether you are an educator, immigrant, refugee, or simply interested in language education, the information provided in this book is valuable for everyone in the pursuit of language proficiency and intercultural understanding.

www.ingramcontent.com/pod-product-compliance
Lightning Source LLC
Chambersburg PA
CBHW061643130726

47996CB00003B/1433